Hosea

UNIT MCCCNT007

Hosea
UNIT 7

Produced by Morling College

Morling College
First Published 2016
122 Herring Rd Macquarie Park NSW 2113 Australia
Phone: +61 2 9878 0201
Email: enquiries@morling.edu.au
www.morlingcollege.com

© Morling College 2016

The publication is copyright. Other than for the purposes of study and subject to the conditions of the Copyright Act, no part of it in any form or by any means (electronic, mechanical, micro-copying, photocopying or otherwise) may be reproduced, stored in a retrieval system or transmitted without the permission of the publisher.

Scripture quotations are from The Holy Bible, New International Version® (NIV®), copyright© 2011 by Biblica, Inc.® Used by permission. All rights reserved worldwide.

ISBN: 978-0-9945725-4-7
Designed by Brugel Images & Design **www.brugel.com.au**
Cover image designed by Freepik.com

Contents

Overview
About the LENS
What is the LENS?. vii
How much time will I need?. . .vii
What Units are in the series?. . .vii
What should I expect in each topic?. viii
Prayer viii
Before we start. viii
Study. viii
Discussion Questions. ix
Demonstrate. ix
Notes: ix

Topic 1
Hosea the prophet and his time
Before we start. 1
Study. 2
Prayer 6
Discussion Questions. 7
Demonstrate. 7
Notes: Topic 1. 8

Topic 2
Hosea's Marriage
Before we start. 9
Study. 9
Prayer 12
Discussion Questions. 13
Demonstrate. 13
Notes: Topic 2. 14

Topic 3
Hosea 1—3
Before we start. 15
Study. 15
Prayer 22
Discussion Questions. 23
Demonstrate. 23
Notes: Topic 3. 24

Topic 4
Hosea 4
Before we start. 25
Study. 26
Prayer 30
Discussion Questions. 31
Demonstrate. 31
Notes: Topic 4. 32

Topic 5
Hosea 5:1—6:6
Before we start. 33
Study. 34
Prayer 38
Discussion Questions. 39
Demonstrate. 39
Notes: Topic 5. 40

Topic 6
Hosea 6:7—7:16
Before we start. 41
Study. 42
Prayer 46
Discussion Questions. 47
Demonstrate. 47
Notes: Topic 6. 48

Topic 7
Hosea 8—9

    Before we start 49
    Study 50
    Prayer 54
    Discussion Questions 55
    Demonstrate 55
    Notes: Topic 7 56

Topic 8
Hosea 10

    Before we start 57
    Study 57
    Prayer 61
    Discussion Questions 62
    Demonstrate 62
    Notes: Topic 8 63

Topic 9
Hosea 11—12

    Before we start 65
    Study 66
    Prayer 70
    Discussion Questions 71
    Demonstrate 71
    Notes: Topic 9 72

Topic 10
Hosea 13—14

    Before we start 73
    Study 73
    Prayer 77
    Discussion Questions 78
    Demonstrate 78
    Notes: Topic 10 79

List of References

    81

Overview

About the LENS

What is the LENS?

The LENS is specifically designed for people who don't wish to complete high-level, accredited study but are keen to access a wide variety of free Bible resources and to engage in a practical Bible study that is free, flexible, and fun.

How much time will I need?

Following the suggested schedule, each Unit will require approximately 5 hours of study each week (meaning roughly 50 hours of study time in total to complete a Unit).

What Units are in the series?

1. Introduction to the Books of the New Testament
2. Mark's Gospel
3. Paul's Letter to the Ephesians
4. The Person and Work of Christ
5. Introduction to the Books of the Old Testament 1
6. Introduction to the Books of the Old Testament 2
7. Hosea
8. Jeremiah

What should I expect in each topic?

Listed below are the sections you will find in each topic, as well as an overview about what you can expect to find in each section.

 Prayer

At the end of each topic is a prayer that helps you to focus on what you are learning.

 Before we start

Each topic begins with an overview that helps you understand what the study is about and gives some background and insight into some of the issues that will be explored during the study.

 Study

This is where the learning happens. By reading these sections thoroughly and thoughtfully, you will grow in your knowledge of the topic. Taking notes and completing the suggested readings (which can be found on Moodle) will allow you to explore the topics more fully.

Overview — About the LENS

 Discussion Questions

If you are participating in the LENS as a part of a group, these questions will help facilitate discussion. Simply pick out a few questions that you think your group will find helpful and interesting, and if time permits you can select some more.

 Demonstrate

For those participating in the LENS for credit, each topic has a Demonstrate section. After completing three Demonstrate questions (from your choice of topics), simply submit your responses via the "Assessment" tab on the Unit's Morling Online Page.

 Notes

You can use this section to write down any of your thoughts about the study.

Topic 1

Hosea the prophet and his time

 ## Before we start

The historical background to Hosea shows us the consequences that result from Israel's sin. Without this we would not understand the full weight of Hosea's prophecy. In many ways Hosea's life is an object lesson for the people of Israel. He is a living expression of God's forbearance and love for his people.

The people of Israel were now a nation. They had been redeemed from slavery in Egypt and been given the law. They were committed to a life of obedience to God, and a religion which constantly reminded them of their dependence on God's forgiveness and mercy. But they were constantly falling down on their calling and promises, through idol-worship, civil war, immorality and complacency. The nation needed to be reminded again and again about their calling from God.

 Study

Old Testament Prophets

Prophets were people raised up by God to call the people back to God and his way. The prophet's calling was not hereditary unlike that of the priests and God chose his prophets from many different walks of life. Some, like Jeremiah and Jonah, were very reluctant recruits, especially when they learnt what God wanted them to do. Out of their relationship with God (see 1 Kings 17:1) the prophets spoke God's message for their contemporaries and beyond (see Acts 7:38). Sometimes they emphasised their message by means of dramatic action, but mostly they presented it in carefully prepared discourses.

Three Hebrew words are translated 'prophet'. The most common one, navi has the idea of 'one who passes on a message from God'. God called them to speak for him, a call which was not an invitation but an appointment. There are two other Hebrew words used of prophets (*roeh, hozeh*), and they are both translated 'seer' meaning 'one who sees'. By God's inspiration the prophets have a unique ability to 'see'; both into the affairs of humans and into the mind of God. Prophecy included prediction of future events, and the fulfilment of these gave the prophet greater authority (see Deut 18:22). But more importantly the prophet had to speak God's word to his people in their current situation.

Hosea the Person

Hosea was one of the four main prophets of the 8th century BC, the others being Amos, Isaiah, and Micah. Like his contemporary, Amos, his message was directed mainly to the ten tribes who formed the northern kingdom Israel, while Micah and Isaiah preached to the southern kingdom Judah. His book is one of 'The book of the Twelve' in the Hebrew Canon, the last book in the Nevi'im (the Prophets). It is also called one of the Minor Prophets - not because it is of lesser importance but because of its shorter length.

Apart from his complex domestic relationships, little is told us of Hosea's personal life. The superscription of 1:1 tells us his father's name, Beeri, whom we cannot positively identify, and dates his prophecy to the second half of the 8th century. Many critics consider the reference to the kings of Judah as a later, inaccurate, editorial addition. However, treating it as a genuine part of the text, we can use it to date Hosea's ministry as commencing before the death of Jeroboam II in 746 BC and continuing at least until the fall of Samaria in 722 BC and possibly extending after the accession of Hezekiah to the throne of Judah in 715 BC.

Russian icon of the prophet Hosea, 18th century (Iconostasis of Transfiguration Church, Kizhi monastery, Karelia, Russia).

The Book of Hosea

The material in Hosea is unique among the Prophetic Books in its division into two distinct parts. Chapters 1-3, the first part, serve as an introduction and deal with Hosea's marriage and its connection to Israel's relationship with God. Chapters 4-14, the second part, are composed of a number of independent discourses.

Social Background

Hosea begins his ministry in some of the most prosperous days in the history of Israel and lives through to see the collapse of the kingdom and its final destruction at the hands of the Assyrians. Amos and Hosea reflect the problems associated with the prosperity of the age. Some of these are:

1. The disappearance of the small peasant farmer and the rise of a wealthy group of absentee landlords. Deprived of their land, peasants often either starved or were sold into slavery to pay their debts (Isa 5:8; Mic 2:1-2; Amos 2:6,7; 5:11). The contrasting luxurious extravagance of the wealthy is reflected in Amos 3:15; 4:1; 5:11; 6:4-6 and Isa 3:14-24.

2. The pollution of religion by the incorporation into worship of many elements of Baal worship (see Hos 2:13, 16-17; 4:13; 11:2) and the failure to give religion moral and ethical associations. Their love of this false worship only alienated God (Hos 8:11-13). Hosea's complaint is that the people are ignorant of the true nature of God and his demands upon them (Hos 2:8; 4:6).

3. Social and moral evil abounded (Hos 4:1-3). The law courts were corrupt (Amos 5:11; 6:12). Business malpractice was common (Amos 8:4-6), and promiscuity was encouraged by religious practices (Amos 2:7; Hos 4:14; 9:2).

Within the apparent prosperity, then, were the seeds of the collapse of the nation.

Historical Background

Jeroboam's death in 746 BC was followed by the murder of his son Zechariah after only six months rule. Zechariah's assassin Shallum was assassinated a month later by Menahem who held control till 737 BC by sheer brutality. The rising Assyrian menace under Tiglath-Pileser forced Menahem to pay a very heavy tribute to Assyria. Menahem virtually surrendered his country's independence so that he might be assured of Assyrian support to keep him on the throne. His son Pekahiah succeeded him but within a short time was murdered by Pekah who became the fifth king of Israel in the ten years since Jeroboam's death, and the third to seize the throne by violence. Pekah joined Rezin, King of Syria, in an anti-Assyrian alliance but in 734 BC Tiglath-Pileser crushed the alliance. Before Samaria itself could be destroyed, Hoshea murdered Pekah and surrendered to Assyria. Hoshea ruled as an Assyrian vassal from 732 to 724 BC but on Tiglath-Pileser's death revolted and tried to form an alliance with Egypt which led to the new Assyrian king, Shalmanezer, attacking and capturing Hoshea. Sargon II succeeded Shalmanezer, who died before the campaign was completed, and captured and destroyed Samaria, deporting its inhabitants in 721 BC. After that Israel ceased to exist as a nation.

Hosea preached against the background of these turbulent days. The upheaval is reflected in the following passages: Hos 5:10-13; 7:7,11; 8:4; 9:15-16; 10:3-6; 12:1; 13:1-11. Hosea's preaching carried a strong note of judgement on the sins of the people but intertwined with that was the expression of the yearning love of God for his disobedient people.[1] This doubtless owed its origins to Hosea's own love for his wife, a subject which will be considered in our next study. It is important that from our study today we see the situation in which Hosea lived and preached and understand the prophetic insight which interpreted the disasters of the later years as God's punishment for the sins of the more prosperous but apostate days which preceded them.

---

1   This contrasts with Amos' tougher approach.

Hosea

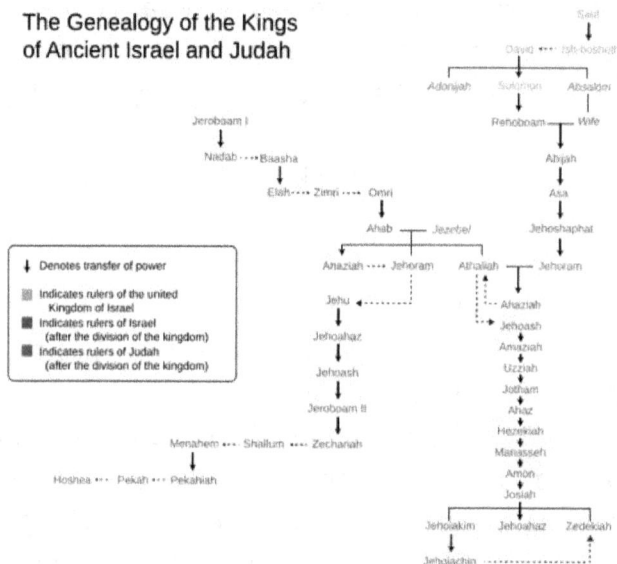

Hosea's prophecy is one of judgement and grace. It contains stern judgement on the one hand and expresses the yearning desire of God that his people should repent on the other. It also presents us with a plain picture of the dangers of prosperity and the self-reliance and self-deceit that can arise from them. Hosea draws a direct line from the sinfulness expressed in the years of Israel's prosperity to the trouble which followed.

Prayer

Dear Lord,

studying the ancient history of Israel can seem very removed from our lives today. And yet in these pages we learn about who you are, God, and how you relate to your people. We pray you will use this study to deepen our knowledge of you and relationship with you.

Amen

Topic 1 — Hosea the prophet and his time

 Discussion Questions

1. Explain the terms 'prophet' and 'prophecy'.
2. What were the social and moral problems in Israel in the time of Hosea?
   (Isa 3:14-24, 5:8; Mic 2:1-2, Amos 2:6-7, 3:15, 4:1, 5:11, 6:4-6, Hos 4:1-3,14 Amos 2:7; 5:11-12; 8:4-6)
3. What was wrong with Israel's religion at the time of Hosea's ministry? See Hos 2:8, 13, 16-17: 4:6, 13; 8:11, 13; 11:2.
4. Why did Israel go through so many kings in a short time, and what does this say to us about human use of power?
5. What social, moral and religious evils are prevalent in society today?
6. What problems do we see with human use of power?

 Demonstrate

What is the situation to which Hosea will bring his prophecy? Describe with reference to both social and political events.

 Notes: Topic 1

Hosea the prophet and his time

Topic 2
Hosea's Marriage

 ## Before we start

Hosea's domestic situation is a living illustration of the relationship between God and rebellious Israel. He marries a woman who betrays him regularly, with all the shame and hurt that must create.

 ## Study

Hosea and History

The interpretation of the first three chapters of Hosea and the picture they reveal of Hosea's relationship with his wife is a matter for some debate. Chapter 1 is written in the third person. In 1:2-3 we are told that Hosea was commanded to take a "promiscuous woman" (NIV),[1] Gomer daughter of Diblaim, who bore him three children whom he called by the symbolic names of *Jezreel* (God sows, 1:4), *Lo-Ruhamah* (not loved, 1:6) and *Lo-Ammi* (not my people, 1:9). Chapter 2 contains preaching by Hosea concerned with Israel's unfaithfulness to God. It also reveals Hosea's

---

1 Note that unless otherwise stated, the version used is NIV 2011.

disturbed relationship with his wife who has presumably been false to him (2:2-5). Chapter 3 appears to again take up Hosea's personal story, this time in the first person. Gomer apparently had left Hosea for her lovers and may even have become a temple prostitute. Hosea is compelled to seek her out and bring her back to their home where she undergoes a period of some form of restriction before restoration to normal family life again (3:1-5). Perhaps the preaching of 2:6-7,13-23 also reflects this restoration.

What are we to make of this strange story? Despite some scholars who, perhaps to avoid the moral issues, have interpreted it in some non-literal way, the majority of modern evangelical commentators view the story as a factual account of Hosea's real experiences. Those who attempt to interpret the story allegorically find difficulty in finding a meaning for such details as the name of Hosea's wife, the sex of the children, the exact price of Gomer's redemption, and the weaning of one child before the birth of the next. Thus, it is better to interpret the story as having a basis in reality.

Did God ask Hosea to sin?

Does "promiscuous woman" mean an acknowledged prostitute or adulteress who was known by Hosea to be promiscuous before marriage? If so does this mean God is demanding his prophet to do an unethical thing? Some suggest the story is a dream or vision while others suggest it is an allegory with no substance in fact. But what is unethical in practice is equally unethical in allegory or vision. Others suggest the names of the children mean that the second and third children are recognised by Hosea to be not his own, but this again assumes the prophet to act in a manner inconsistent with his vocation in apparently countenancing Gomer's infidelity by continuing to live with her.

There have been various ways of resolving this difficulty. Some suggest that she is spoken of as promiscuous, because she will become so. Others that like any other Israelite woman, she is metaphorically promiscuous because she is idolatrous. However, Hosea could be indeed called to show love towards this promiscuous woman.[2]

Out of this tragic story God brought a good thing. It was doubtless in his realisation of his own love for his wife, despite her unfaithfulness to him, that Hosea perceived that God could love an Israel who was unfaithful.

Hosea's Suffering

Illustration of Hosea and Gomer from the Bible Historiale, 1372.

The suffering Hosea underwent gives us insight into God's love for Israel. Such a cry as is expressed in 11:1-4,8 grows out of Hosea's deeply personal experiences with Gomer.

Hosea's life thus becomes a sermon in itself. The most distinctive notes in his teaching have their origin in his personal experience. His proclamation of the love of God which persists despite human sin and unfaithfulness, receives its full expression in the life and teaching of Jesus.

---

2 See the good discussion in J. Andrew Dearman, *The Book of Hosea, The New International Commentary on the Old Testament* (Grand Rapids, Michigan: Eerdmans, 2010), 84-88.

Hosea is a unique book that inextricably intertwines the life of the prophet with the message of judgement and God's love. In it we see a living example of the pain suffered by God and the willingness of God to rescue his fallen people.

Prayer

Dear Lord,

We are tempted to underestimate both your holiness and your love. This story of Hosea and Gomer gives us a moving example of the depth of the love of our holy God for his people. Please help us to glimpse that love, and to give that love ourselves to your people.

Amen

Topic 2 — Hosea's Marriage

 Discussion Questions

1. How did Hosea use his own personal experiences to understand God's message and will? (Hos 1-3)
2. How do you understand what Hosea was told to do in 1:2?
3. What was the significance of the name Jezreel for Hosea's first child? (Hos 1:4). What promise did the name hold? (1:11)
4. What would be the effect of the reversal of the names in verses 1:10—2:1?
5. Through Hosea God is giving Israel a last opportunity to repent before judgment breaks on the land. What was the judgment that did occur? (2 Kings 17:13-23)
6. What relevance has the experience of Hosea to the Christian understanding of God's relationship with humanity?

 Demonstrate

Hosea described the relationship between God and his people as that of husband and wife. Why do you think Hosea and other prophets used human comparisons when speaking of God?

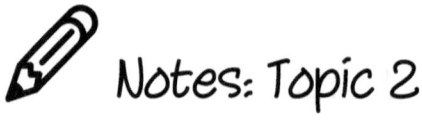

Notes: Topic 2

Hosea's Marriage

Topic 3

Hosea 1-3

Before we start

In our last study we looked at the problem of Hosea's marriage. In this study we will examine the first three chapters in more detail, in which his marriage and family are figured. The names of Hosea's children also play a significant role in the first three chapters of Hosea. Hosea gives his children significant names to illustrate God's intentions towards Israel.

 Study

Hosea 1:1-8

In Hos 1:1, Hosea's prophecy begins with a significant statement; "The word of the Lord that came to Hosea" which may be translated, "The beginning of that which God spoke by Hosea". God was not only speaking to Hosea but through him to others. The nation he spoke to was deaf to his appeals and was sent into exile. But his message was preserved and passed on, and succeeding generations have been blessed by it. Thus Hosea's ministry was certainly not in vain.

Verses 1-3 have been discussed in the first and second studies. As we move to 4-5, a son named Jezreel is mentioned. Jezreel (literally 'God sows') is the name of the valley in which Naboth's vineyard was located (1 Kings 21:1) and where Jehu murdered Joram (2 Kings 9). The significance of the name is that Jehu's dynasty will also be terminated in bloodshed (2 Kings 15:8-12), but as verse 5 indicates not only would the house of Jehu be judged but the military power of Israel would be broken when God's judgment came "in that day". That Day, or the Day, are terms used by the prophets to refer to a future time when God will visit his people in final blessing and/or judgment.

In verses 6-7 a daughter Lo-ruhamah (not loved) is born. Her name is referenced in Rom 9:25 and 1 Pet 2:10 where it is rendered, respectively, 'not my loved one' and 'not received mercy.' Her name served to indicate to the people of Israel that they could expect no mercy from God. As the 'unloved one' she symbolised the plight of the Northern Kingdom of Israel which had sinned against God and was ripe for judgment. Verse 7 is one of the many side-glances at Judah, some favourable as in this verse (compare with 1:11, 4:15, 11:12), others unfavourable (5:5, 10-14; 6:4-11; 8:14; 10:11; 12:2). However, the general sense is clear; Judah will escape the judgment (Judah lasted 130 years after Samaria's collapse) but Israel is doomed to a quicker destruction. The reference to Judah's method of deliverance here may be connected with the story in 2 Kings 19:35.

In verses 8-9 another son, Lo-ammi (not my people) is born. His name is taken by some to imply that Hosea thought the child wasn't his but it need not be seen that way. Rather, as with the other names, it can be viewed as symbolic, here of a rejection by God of Israel as his covenant people. 'I am not your God' is a direct reversal of Exod 3:14 - literally 'Not God to you'. At Sinai Israel had covenanted to be God's people and he would be their God (Exod 19:1-8), but Israel repeatedly broke that covenant, so Hosea declares that they will be rejected. This rejection will result in exile and the destruction of the Kingdom of Israel as a political entity.

There is possibly an ascending scale in the prediction of Israel's doom with each child: Jezreel, an announcement of coming judgement; Lo-ruhamah, the withdrawal of God's love; Lo-ammi, Israel's ejection from the covenant relationship.

Hosea 1:10—2:1

The Hebrew Bible ends chapter 1 with verse 9 and begins its second chapter with verse 10. These verses, by contrast with the preceding ones, carry a message of hope and restoration. The people of Israel will increase to immeasurable numbers and the old covenant relationship with God will be restored.

Judgment deserved is matched by mercy undeserved, to the extent that the latter blessings surpass the former. An innumerable company "like the sand" was originally promised in the covenant with Abraham and reiterated to Jacob (Gen 22:15-18; 28:13-15, compare with Rev 7:9).

The kingdoms of Judah and Israel will be reunited under one leader. Some see this as a political union; others see it as a future hope yet to be realised; whilst others transfer this promise to the Church. Certainly, centuries later Jesus is spoken of as unifying the people of God under himself (Heb 8:7-8; Eph 3:6).

'The day of Jezreel' in verse 11 is perhaps a reference to some future victory to be won by the Israelites in battle at Jezreel but more likely a reference to the meaning of Jezreel ('God sows'). Jezreel becomes, instead of a place of judgment, a promise of the outpouring of God's blessing, the place where God would once again sow Israel with the seed of life.

Hosea 2:2-13

Bronze figurine of a Baal, 14th - 12th century BCE, found at Ras Shamra (ancient Ugarit) near the Phoenician coast. Musée du Louvre.

This passage uses the example of Hosea's wife Gomer and her faithless conduct and pursuit of her lovers as a metaphor for Israel's worship of the baals. It is unclear whether this is a formal divorce or just a separation.[1] The children of verse 2 are therefore both Gomer's children and the individual Israelites who will suffer for the sins of the nation, mother Israel. The whole passage is one of grim warning of the inevitability of punishment for apostasy mingled with the frustrated longing of the forsaken husband (thus 'plead', v2, and the sad cry of v8). Note also that the intention of punishment is to bring about restoration (vv6-7).

Verses 5 and 8 suggest a contemporary parallel for discussion. Are we not also in danger of attributing our material gains to our own abilities? We only pay lip service, if that, to God as the "giver of every good and perfect gift" (James 1:17 compare with Judg 7:2).

The response of the husband, in this case God, described here has three phases:

---

[1] See the discussion in J. Andrew Dearman, *The Book of Hosea, The New International Commentary on the Old Testament* (Grand Rapids, Michigan: Eerdmans, 2010), 109.

1. The husband will block the wife's way to her lovers (Israel's pursuit of idols, vv6-7)
2. The husband will take away the wife's spousal provision, the result being she will have nothing to clothe herself with, and will be exposed (vv9, 12). This is particularly apt for God as the Lord of Nature rather than the baals.
3. Here the focus is shifting much more to Israel and God, away from the Hosea's marriage. God says he will move their festivals, because they worshipped the baals (vv11-13).

Hosea 2:14-23

Just as 1:10—2:1 provided a promise of mercy against the background of the judgement found in 1:2-9, so these verses speak of the establishment of a new marriage bond and a new covenant in contrast to the judgment picture of 2:2-13.

Verse 14: God appears as a lover who woos Israel away from false lovers ('speak tenderly', compare with Ruth 2:13, Gen. 34:3, Is. 40:2), and takes Israel back to the wilderness, the symbol of the days when Israel first became betrothed to God.

Verse 15: the phrase 'Valley of Achor' – refers to the scene of Achan's sin in Joshua 7:24, but also the way into the promised land so that here it contains a promise of restoration. These two verses look back to the wilderness experience of Exodus as the time when Israel's relationship to God was pure before the influence of Canaanite worship led Israel into apostasy.

Verse 16: While in some way it seems that Hosea and Gomer are no longer husband and wife (v2), the relationship will be restored. There is also a play on the meaning of Baal which as well as being the false gods, also means, 'Lord, master, husband'. By extension, the proper relationship between Israel and God would also be restored.

Verse 17: That is, God's people will worship only God.

Verse 18: The promise of universal peace and harmony between humans and animals is a common Messianic picture. It is a way of imaging the peace that will exist when the Messiah is in complete control (compare with Isa 11:6-9; Isa 2:2-4).

Verses 19-20: Again the ethical qualities of love and justice, which are here expressed in terms of the marriage relationship, are typical of the right relationships which still exist between humanity and God and humans with each other in the Messianic age. Note the contrast with the apostasy and unfaithfulness of that time.

Verses 21-22: Nature is involved in the future blessing just as it was involved in the judgment (2:9,12). Material prosperity is a part of Old Testament Messianic thinking.

Verse 23: the name Jezreel alludes to the name of Hosea's firstborn but here anticipates the name change, and has the positive meaning of 'God plants' promising abundant harvest. As Garrett says, "The name Jezreel had meant calamity for Israel (1:4-5) but now it implies salvation and prosperity."[2] Similarly the reversal of the other names, as in 1:10 and 2:1, shows the completeness of the restoration of Israel.

Hosea 3:1-5

Here the personal story of Hosea and Gomer is resumed. Under God's leading Hosea seeks out Gomer, buys her freedom and restores her to his household but under certain unspecified restrictions. It has been variously suggested Hosea pays her debts, or she had sold herself into slavery or temple prostitution.

---

[2] Duane A. Garrett, *Hosea, Joel*, The New American Commentary (Nashville, Tennessee: Broadman & Holman, 1997), 95.

See the discussion in Garrett and Dearman.[3]

Verse 1: Hosea's love for Gomer is directly paralleled to God's love for Israel. The phrase 'love the sacred raisin cakes' is descriptive of Baal worshippers who offered raisin cakes to Baal as part of the harvest thanksgiving festival. Also dried grapes were used in the worship of fertility gods, who were believed to give abundant harvests to their worshippers.

Verse 2: Hosea pays for Gomer both with money and in kind. It is unclear why this is. See discussion above.

Verse 3: "Remain as mine" (NRSV), "live with me" (NIV) - the verb means 'live in seclusion' i.e. be denied normal conjugal rights for a period as punishment for her unfaithfulness.

Verses 4-5: God will treat disloyal Israel as Hosea treated his wife. The people will go into captivity before the full covenant relationship is restored. They will live "without king or prince, without sacrifice or sacred stones, without ephod or household gods." According to Garrett, all except for the household gods (idols) are in themselves neutral.[4] The sacred stones and ephod can also be used in worship of God. However, all in the list have been corrupted by the idolatry of Israel. The meaning here is that Israel will be deprived, at least temporarily, of their leadership and means of worship.

---

[3] Gary V. Smith, *Hosea, Amos, Micah : The NIV Application Commentary from Biblical Text to Contemporary Life,* The NIV Application Commentary Series (Grand Rapids, Mich.: Zondervan Pub. House, 2001), 74. Garrett, Hosea, Joel, 101; Dearman, *The Book of Hosea*, 135.

[4] Garrett, *Hosea, Joel*, 103.

Summary

These three chapters form the background for the rest of the book. The remainder consists of sermons preached by Hosea warning of judgment to come upon God's apostate people but containing promises of a future restoration. The warmly human character of the man seen in the intimacy of chapters 1 and 3 may also be seen emerging in the message he brings through his prophecy.

Israel was no longer placing their trust in God and was actively seeking out substitutes for God in their national life and their private lives. In this way they had become like an unfaithful wife selling herself for the illusory protection of other men, not realising that these substitute husbands would either fail to provide security or would ultimately treat her as a slave.

Prayer

Dear Lord,

Like the people of Israel, we put our trust in many inferior substitutes instead of you. Please show us what we leaning on instead of you, and help us to rest instead on you.

Amen

Topic 3 — Hosea 1—3

 Discussion Questions

1. What did God promise Abraham in the original covenant? (Gen 22:15-18). What was the Israelite people's responsibility in the covenant agreement? (Exod 19:1-8).

2. How are the promises of Hos 1:10—2:1 fulfilled by the Church? (John 1:12,13, Gal 6:16; Rom 9:22-26, 1 Pet 2:9-10, Rev 7:9).

3. In Hos 2:3-13 Gomer is punished as Israel will be punished by exile. What is the purpose of these punishments and what may be the purpose of punishment or discipline we receive from God? (Hebrews 12:7-11). What is the attitude of the one inflicting the punishment?

4. What will a renewed 'marriage' between God and his people look like (2:18-23)?

5. What do Hosea's actions in chapter 3 tell us about God's relationship with Israel?

6. What inferior substitutes for God do people lean on in our society today?

 Demonstrate

How does Hosea's personal situation give us insight into God's relationship with Israel?

 Notes: Topic 3

Hosea 1—3

Topic 4
Hosea 4

 ## Before we start

Hosea's main point in this chapter is the failure of God's people to know God. The failure to know God as he really is results in lowered moral and ethical standards (4:2). This is a particularly relevant issue today when there is an attempt to replace religious faith with an ethic which has no religious grounding.

The brief oracle in 4:1-3 is a prophetic speech form called 'judgment speech'. (compare with Hos 2:2, Mic 6:1ff, Isa 1:18ff). The source of this form is found in the legal procedure practised in Israel's courts, and its use has the effect of putting the entire nation on trial with God serving as both prosecutor and judge.

 Study

Hosea 4:1

Charge *(rib)*: a legal word suggesting a complaint or charge in a law case.

Specifically, all of Israel are accused of a lack of 'faithfulness', 'love' and 'knowledge of God'. All 3 are covenantal terms and must be understood in that context. Dearman points out that faithfulness and love are attributes of God, so to fail in them reveals a lack of knowledge of God.[1]

Faithfulness *(emeth)*: emeth means both truth and faithfulness - so not only in speaking what is right, but also doing what is right. Your relationship with God affects your relationship with others. People can live with neither God nor humans if their relationship with God is devoid of faithfulness.[2]

Love *(hesed)*: In older translations this appears as 'kindness' which in popular usage is a rather weak word, connoting a mild type of consideration and concern for others. Yet the word used here *(hesed)* is a strong word meaning 'steadfast love' or 'covenant love', which speaks of a relationship between those who have accepted mutual obligations in a spirit of trust and love.[3]

---

1 Dearman, *The Book of Hosea*, 147. Strong's number 7379, definition: a contest (personal or legal):— adversary, cause, chiding, contend(-tion), controversy, multitude (from the margin), pleading, strife, strive(-ing), suit.
2 Strong's number 571, definition: stability; (figuratively) certainty, truth, trustworthiness:—assured(-ly), establishment, faithful, right, sure, true (-ly, -th), verity.
3 Strong's number 2617, definition: kindness; by implication (towards God) piety; rarely (by opposition) reproof, or (subjectively) beauty:—favour, good deed(-liness, -ness), kindly, (loving-) kindness, merciful (kindness), mercy, pity, reproach, wicked thing.

Knowledge *(daath)* of God: For Hosea, knowing God is much more than a passive acquaintance or an intellectual knowledge. It is an intimate experience; a personal relationship. The root evil named in God's accusation against his people is their lack of a 'knowledge of God'.[4]

Hosea 4:2

The five crimes named in this verse are more than simple violations of general morality. They are acts prohibited by God in his covenant. These acts of swearing, lying, killing, stealing, committing adultery, violated five of the Ten Commandments; the five most directly related to a person's relationship with other people (Exod 20:1-17).

Hosea 4:3

The land is depicted as closely connected to the people, and so the land also feels the effect of sin. The land is part of God's covenant with Israel. Human sin has an effect on nature (see also Amos 8:8, Joel 1:10-12 and Rom 8:22). One obvious modern parallel of sin affecting nature is the devastation left behind in warfare, another is greed for more money causing destruction of forests, and most obviously our over consumption leading to climate change.

Hosea 4:4-6

Hosea locates some of the blame for Israel's failings in their leadership, which demonstrates the importance of faithful leaders.

---

[4] Strong's number 1847 knowledge:—cunning, (ig-) norantly, know(-ledge), (un-) awares (wittingly).

"I will destroy your mother" (v5) may refer to the destruction of the capital city, or the nation. The prophets of verse 5 are false prophets, probably attached to the temple shrines at Bethel and elsewhere in Samaria. It is probable that worship at these shrines was a mixture of Canaanite and God worship with some temple prostitution. This reflected a failure to understand God as a God who was himself moral and who demanded morality from his worshippers. This rejection by the priests of the true knowledge of God will result in God in turn rejecting the priests and the nation i.e. no longer protecting them as his own.

Hosea 4:7-8

As the priesthood increased in wealth and numbers, they deteriorated as religious leaders and debased the glories of their calling. They used their office for personal profit, delighting in the sin of the people since such sin meant sacrificial offerings, which in turn became the priests' personal property (compare with Lev 6:14-30; 7:6-10, for the relevant laws).

Hosea 4:9-10

Both priests and people will share in a common punishment and find no satisfaction from their wickedness.

Hosea 4:11-14

Although the people may have been misled, their own sins were considerable. Drunkenness (v11) idolatry (vv12-13) and immorality with sacred prostitutes at the shrines (vv13-14) are prevalent.

In verse 12 the 'staff' or 'stick' refers to some form of divination in which a stick is thrown in order to secure (from the way it falls) the answer of the deity (compare with Ezek 21:21f). In verse 14, though adulteresses were severely dealt with in Israel (see Lev 20:10), Hosea declares that the Lord will not punish the daughters and brides for their illicit deeds. This is because the men are also involved in the sin. These verses argue against a double standard, in which women are blamed and men go unpunished. Instead, as Smith says, the contribution of men who "set up, promote and probably demand this perverse sexual activity" is recognised.[5]

Hosea 4:15-19

These verses (and also 1:7,11; 4:15; 5:10-14; 8:14) view Judah in a favourable light. Hosea had an intimate knowledge of the conditions in the Kingdom of Judah and a deep concern for Judah. Also, in the prophet's warnings and promises to Judah there was a message for Israel, if Israel would only listen and act.

Hosea's warning to Judah is a threefold one:

1. Judah should not become like Israel in worshipping idols (v17).
2. Judah is not to become like Israel by wilfully disobeying God (v16 - like a stubborn heifer).
3. Judah is to leave Israel alone (v17). In verse 17 there occurs Hosea's first use of the name 'Ephraim' for Israel. Ephraim was the largest and most important tribe of the ten included in the northern kingdom of Israel. Hosea uses this term 37 times.

The phrase 'Beth-aven' is probably a corruption of Beth-el, 'House of God' to 'Beth-aven', 'House of Iniquity'. Gilgal and Bethel were two of the major Israelite shrines where taking an oath on God's name is a blasphemy.

---

[5] Smith, *Hosea, Amos, Micah : The Niv Application Commentary from Biblical Text to Contemporary Life*, 87.

The wind in verse 19 is probably a reference to the Assyrian conqueror who will carry Israel into captivity, an all-enveloping irresistible force. Their confidence in this false worship will prove groundless and will lead to their open shame.

The key verse in chapter 4 is verse 6. The idolatry and licentiousness of the people all bear testimony to their failure to understand God's nature and his love. Finally, he is left with no alternative. Despite his love, punishment must fall, though with an ultimate goal of redemption.

The love of God for Israel and Israel's unfaithfulness to God remains at the centre of this entire series of oracles. The descriptions that Hosea employs to illustrate Israel's sins are those of a marriage covenant breaking up, before switching to a form of legal speech that places the entire nation on trial with God serving as both prosecutor and judge. By failing to understand God as he really is, Israel has lowered its moral and ethical standards and brought judgement upon it. This stands as a severe warning against the modern tendency to try to ground morality in a non-religious ethic.

Prayer

Dear Lord,

The way we act as your people betrays that we don't know you as well as we should. Help us to seek your face, to come to know you better and better, so that we might be like you in the world.

Amen

Topic 4 — Hosea 4

 Discussion Questions

1. Compare and contrast Israel and Judah as described by Hosea in this chapter.
2. Imagine you are a prosecutor bringing charges against the Israelites.
    - What are the charges being brought against Israel?
    - What crime/s have they committed?
    - What is the evidence?
3. Why is the priestly corruption particularly problematic?
4. How does the way the people worship betray that they don't know God?
5. Is it true that sin never satisfies? Compare with Eccles 2:10,11.
6. Are there areas of hypocrisy in your life? What practical steps can you take to address them?

 Demonstrate

Why does inadequate knowledge of God lead to sin? Answer with reference to the book of Hosea.

 Notes: Topic 4

Hosea 4

Topic 5

Hosea 5:1–6:6

 ## Before we start

Decrying the nearness of the end has become something of a caricature in our society today. The individual with the placard warning us of the end is someone to be mocked; not someone to take seriously.

The prophets of God in the history of Israel were also often met with scorn and derision. In Hosea's era, people felt secure in their wealth and well-being. They thought it laughable that they could lose all they had put their trust in and be genuinely called to account for their actions and lifestyles. Hosea's warning went unheeded and terrible calamity followed.

The next three chapters deal with issues involving every section of the community and every aspect of national life. The leaders of the nation are condemned for their violation of the covenant and their wanton acts of sin.

 Study

Hosea 5:1-2

Chapter 5 begins with the condemnation of the priests and the princes who are considered to be responsible for the serious plight of the country. What evil deeds had occurred at Mizpah, Tabor and Shittim we are not told but probably some pagan cult was operating at each centre. Certainly the allusion to these places would refer to something well known to Hosea's listeners. Three ways to catch wild animals are named in relation to the locations: snare, net and pit. These represent the seduction to idolatry by which people were caught when they thought they were worshipping the Lord.

In verse 2 Hosea uses the word 'punish' or 'chastise'. The Hebrew word used is also used in the context of teaching and its discipline. Thus, Hosea suggests the idea of a redemption which is grounded in discipline. Though the leaders have failed and the people are not without fault, God remains their teacher. Through the discipline of history God will teach them the meaning of their status as his people, for whom punishment is not for the purpose of destruction but for salvation and deliverance.

Hosea 5:3-4

Israel have been alienated from God for so long that they have forgotten what he is like. Moreover, they are so much in bondage to sin they have lost the inclination to return.

Smith gives four reasons why Israel's recovery will be hard:

1. "failures at Mizpah, Tabor and probably Shittim", what they are is unknown, but they have an experience of entrapment.

2. "religious prostitution the priests have encouraged". This makes it difficult to have a relationship with God.
3. "the nation's 'arrogance'". Refusing to admit what they have done wrong
4. "God's abandonment" due to the people's unfaithfulness.[1]

Hosea 5:5-7

When Ephraim and Judah fall they will seek in vain to placate God with their flocks and herds. The illegitimate children are the products of Israel's unfaithfulness. They are children who worship idolatrously without any knowledge of God at all. The new moon, normally a festival of rejoicing, will be a time of judgment. The thought may be that very soon (at the next new moon) the people and the land will be desolated.

Hosea 5:8-14

Tiglath-Pileser III: stela from the walls of his palace (British Museum, London).

This section might be entitled "Cry havoc, and let slip the dogs of war."[2] The alarm is sounded as the foe advances (v8) but no army can stand against God's wrath (v9). The princes who apparently have been guilty of interfering with time honoured property rights (compare Deut 19:14, 27:17) will receive the full measure of God's anger (v10). Israel will be overthrown and crushed because of

---

[1] Smith, *Hosea, Amos, Micah : The Niv Application Commentary from Biblical Text to Contemporary Life,* 101-02.
[2] Shakespeare, *Julius Caesar,* Act 3, Scene 1, line 273.

preferring to follow idols (v11). Many interpret this passage in terms of the Assyrian king Tiglath-Pileser's invasion of Israel in 733 BC when the country was forced to pay a heavy tribute in acknowledgement of their subjugation.

By contrast with the suddenness of being overthrown, the figures of the moth and dry rot in verse 12 suggest a process of gradual corruption and decay. Sin and judgment sap the strength and glory of a nation little by little. If there really is a sudden collapse, it is like that of a house whose timbers have become empty shells by the attacks of termites.

In this oracle Hosea goes further. It is God who has been eating away the strength of Israel and Judah, like moth and rot. *Ash* can be translated variously as moth, maggots, pus or disease. Coupled with the next word (rot/rottenness) there is an overwhelming sense of deterioration.[3]

This introduces the thought of verse 13 in which Israel, aware of their weakness, appealed to Assyria for help, a probable reference to either Menaham's tribute to Tiglath-Pileser in 738 or Hogshead's subjection to Assyria from 732 to 724 BC. 'The great king' (King Jareb-AV) is a common term of personal reference used by the Assyrian kings in their inscriptions. However, the Assyrians are powerless to help Israel since it is God who is attacking Israel and resistance to him is useless (v14).

Hosea 5:15—6:6

These verses are among the most moving in Hosea's prophecy. God determines to withdraw himself from Israel until he sees evidence of a genuine desire for repentance and renewal of the love bond of the covenant relationship on the part of the Israelites (5:15). But what he sees is only either an apparent or

---

[3] See Dearman, *The Book of Hosea*, 185 and Smith, *Hosea, Amos, Micah : The Niv Application Commentary from Biblical Text to Contemporary Life,* 104.

fleeting repentance - a superficial confidence and false security in God's willingness to protect his people. They assume that divine mercy is at the beck and call of human expressions of repentance, whether genuine or not. For above all there is no indication that the lessons of chapters 1-3 have been understood and assimilated.

God has to tell them that what they lack above all is loyalty (vv4, 6). In a stranger, instability of behaviour may be excusable, but where there is a firm covenant bond, as between Hosea and Gomer, God and Israel, repeated expressions of repentance cannot take the place of the love and loyalty that is expected in the covenant. This does not suggest that there is not forgiveness, but that forgiveness is for the lapse from the covenant, not for its ignoring until the bitterness of circumstances draw a few perfunctory and stereotyped expressions of regret to the lips.

Such a shallow repentance causes God's heart-broken cry of 6:4-6. There is frustration and pathos in the cry "What can I do with you?" (NIV) Israel's covenant loyalty (hesed) was as transitory as a passing cloud or dew in the morning. God has attempted to shape the Israelites through the prophetic teaching and guide by the shining light of the covenant commandments (6:5) but to no avail. Verse 6 is the central verse of the prophecy. It is not ritual observance God desires but instead the right covenant relationships (hesed again) and an intimate personal knowledge of him.

Here we have seen the corruption of the priests and the princes and the terrible consequences coming for the nation. So corrupt has Israel become that it has lost even the desire to truly repent and return to God. As a result, war will soon come upon them in judgment, smashing to pieces the empty optimism they have been espousing.

Prayer

Dear Lord,

We also substitute ritual observance for a real relationship with you. Please show us those aspects of our Christian life which we take false pride in, and humbly turn us back to you.

Amen

Topic 5 – Hosea 5:1—6:6

 Discussion Questions

1. What are the four reasons why Israel cannot return to God?
2. What is the meaning of 'illegitimate children' (NIV) (5:7)?
3. Ephraim and Judah attempt to buy their way back with flocks and herds. Will they succeed? Why/why not?
4. What constitutes genuine repentance?
5. How is genuine repentance different from the repentance being expressed by Israel?
6. How can we resist and oppose the cultural forces pushing our own society towards the same collapse as was experienced by Israel?

 Demonstrate

How do you understand the judgment of chapter 5 in the light of the love of God so clearly portrayed elsewhere in Hosea?

Notes: Topic 5

Hosea 5:1—6:6

Topic 6
Hosea 6:7–7:16

 Before we start

Standing up for what is right comes at a cost. Martin Luther King Jr. was targeted and investigated by the FBI. He was so hated by J. Edgar Hoover that the FBI released details of his marital infidelity to his wife in an attempt to drive him to suicide.

Others who have acted as whistle-blowers and honest dissenters in the face of public and private evils have also faced persecution even from the governments supposedly charged with protecting their rights.

One counterpart we have to prophets in the modern context are whistleblowers and non-violent protesters who seek to draw our attention to the injustices and evils of our own times. Their willingness to announce unpopular truths makes them automatic targets for ridicule and heated opposition. Thinking about how such people are treated gives us a little insight into the way Hosea was received in his own time.

The remainder of Chapters 6 and 7 is a heaping up of Israel's sins.

 Study

Hosea 6:7-11

The sins enumerated in 6:7-10 are presented as evidence that Israel lacks the essential qualities that God requires in relationship with him (6:6). This section is a geography of Israel's sin and guilt. Hosea moves from one location to another as he catalogues the crimes which inflict his beloved country. Interpretation of this section is difficult. Incidents which were infamous in Hosea's day are now unknown or at best uncertain.

Evidence of Israel's crimes can be found at the sanctuaries of Adam, Gilead and Shechem. The use of the word Adam here is difficult but it is probably a place-name (compare with Josh 3:16). The priests are responsible for all sorts of villainy, including the abuse of Shechem, an ancient city of refuge for unintentional murder (Josh 20:7). Immorality, probably associated with temple prostitution, is evident in the house of Israel, which many scholars read as happening at Bethel, the leading shrine. Judah also shares in the wickedness and will reap judgment.

Hosea 7:1-2

God's efforts to heal his people only reveal their guilt more clearly.

Hosea 7:3-7

This section serves admirably as a transition from Israel's moral defections to an inevitable consequence; corrupt political conditions. Both evils are portrayed in these verses.

The king is surrounded by unscrupulous nobles where adultery, drunkenness, conspiracies and assassinations are the rule. No one in the court thinks of appealing to God for guidance. The passage probably reflects conditions about 745 to 737 BC in which three kings, Zechariah, Shallum, and Pekahiah, had all been murdered by their successors and the monarchy and court were obviously corrupt.

In verses 5-7 we see the people anointing the new king and accepting his ministers and the families that swept into power with him, but all the time with lies and treachery in their hearts. Their loyalty lasts as long as their advantage does. Just as the heat of the baker's oven is allowed to moderate until the dough is ready, so their anger is restrained until their time is ripe. Then the treacherous plotters sit at the table of the doomed king plying him with wine until the moment of his assassination.

Hosea 7:8-16

Pekah from Guillaume Rouillé's Promptuarii Iconum Insigniorum

Israel's internal anarchy was matched by faithless foreign policy. In Pekah's rule (737-732 BC) Egyptian aid was sought and during Menahem's (745-738 BC) and Hoshea's rule (732-724 BC) alliances were formed with Assyria and later with Egypt. As God's covenant people, Israel should have turned to him and not to other powers.

It should have been fundamental for Israel that no foreign alliances should be sought. The reason was that in those days the secular state did not exist, and so in practice it was impossible to distinguish between a state and its gods. In a peace treaty between Rameses II of Egypt and Hattusilis, the Hittite king, it is a thousand of their gods on either side who are the witnesses to and guarantors of it. So even a treaty on equal terms with a neighbouring country would have involved for Israel a recognition of the other country's deities as having reality and equality with God. To turn to Assyria or Egypt for help out of necessity implied that their gods were more effective than the God of Israel. This then explains the bitterness of Hosea's attack on Israel's foreign policy in 7:8-16.

The language of verses 4 and 8 leads some to postulate that Hosea was a baker by trade. "A loaf not turned over" (v8) is one only half-baked. So Israel's policy was a combination of half-hearted religion and politics. The people themselves were also attempting to be people of God and people of the world around them. As a result, the national character was fickle and inconsistent, lacking decisiveness and a sense of direction. Some scholars suggest that the English phrase 'half-baked' doesn't quite give the full sense here. We think that something half-baked, with some skill, can be saved and baked through. In this time, however, one side was so overbaked and charred that the whole was fit for nothing. While the visible part was normal, the whole was, in fact, ruined.

In verse 10 the arrogance, 'the pride of Israel', blinds them to their approaching fate. Despite the apparent signs of decay, 'for all this', Israel does not return to God.

Verse 12 is a statement, following the metaphor of verse 11, that God will bring Israel into the trap they had sought to avoid by their political manoeuvrings. Israel is "like a dove", silly and without a sense of understanding, "calling to Egypt, going to Assyria" (v11). The dove was known for its foolishness, largely because of its apparently aimless flight. The people are flitting from alliance to alliance. Hosea considered alliances with either Egypt or Assyria as the rejection of God. But just as the pigeon-owner takes precautions that his birds do not get lost, so God was watching over Israel, not to save them but to punish them. They will land in his net, and he "will bring them down like the birds of the air" (v12).

The longing of God for Israel's return and the continual affront to his love by their failure to do so reoccurs in verses 10, 13 ("I would redeem them, but……"). Again Israel's failure to perceive God as the giver of all good is a reflection of their failure to know and understand his nature (vv14-15). Israel's failure lies in wicked leadership, an easy religion and a reliance on material. Resulting in a nation held up to derision and exiles in a strange land.

Israel's most heinous sin was "turning to Baal" (vv13, 16a). As well as this, instead of petitioning God from their hearts (v14) for grain and wine they slash themselves to appeal to their false gods (compare with 1 Kings 18:26-28). The Israelites thought of God as absent like Baal and sought by various techniques to summon him to get help for their crops. For Israel to seek strength through alliances with Egypt and Assyria and to turn away from God to Baal, was to deny the revelation of God in their history. In turning to Baal Israel was guilty of treachery, like a warped bow that does not shoot straight, whose arrow does not hit the target. Their death will bring derision (v16) from the Egyptians whose help they had alternately sought and scorned.

There is a close correlation between the moral corruption of Israel and its political corruption. Political assassination was frequent and the protection of world powers (and their gods) was sought in place of reliance on God. Worst of all the people were worshipping Baal in place of God. In these passages we have a catalogue of the wholesale turning away from God of God's chosen people.

 Prayer

Dear Lord,

We often pay more attention to our individual sin and ignore the sin we are committing communally – whether as the church or society. Open our eyes to the ways we are involved in systemic sin and help us to be agents of change.

Amen

Topic 6 — Hosea 6:7—7:16

 Discussion Questions

1. 1. This section of Hosea presents a number of similes. List each one and explain the meaning the simile conveys:

Simile	Meaning

2. To whom did Israel turn when aid was required? What did this mean for their relationship with God?
3. Where was Israel's sin leading?
4. What was Israel's most heinous sin?
5. Have you ever had to stand up for what you believe in the face of opposition or known someone who did? What was the result?
6. In what ways does Hosea model the kind of courage and commitment to God that we should emulate?

 Demonstrate

How are moral and political sin related in Hosea, and what does this mean for us and how we live out our faith today?

47

 Notes: Topic 6

Hosea 6:7—7:16

Topic 7
Hosea 8-9

 ## Before we start

In July 1914 Europe descended into the war that became known as the First World War. Europe was awash with treaties and political agreements that were meant to prevent war through pacts of mutual defence, but this structure collapsed and saw numerous countries scrambling to achieve quick victories in an ever widening conflict that lasted years. Prior to the war, many placed their trust in the alliances and agreements between nations to prevent catastrophe but catastrophe (on an unprecedented scale) came anyway.

In many ways this is the same situation that Israel finds itself in, falsely trusting alliances with its neighbours to protect it. When Hosea preaches against this false trust he is laughed to scorn. These two chapters are concerned with the inevitable judgment which will come to Israel for national idolatry and covenant breaking. This judgment will be expressed in warfare and finally exile.

 Study

Hosea 8:1-3

In ancient times the trumpet blast was a sound of warning given by command of one of high authority (compare with 2 Sam 2:28; 18:16; 20:22). In verse 1 the trumpet sounds a clear note of warning to Israel and does so at the command of the highest authority, God himself.

Israel's basic sin has been the breaking of the covenant, that special bond which had existed between Israel and God since the wilderness (Ex. 10:5-6; 24:7-8). The primary breach of the covenant consisted in the substitution of the Canaanite religion for that of God.

The idea of the covenant relationship dominates both Old and New Testament thinking. Israel's rejection of the covenant forces God to act in judgment by sending an invading army (described as a vulture about to swoop; v1). Israel's self-serving attempt to renew relationship with God (v2) is useless since the lives of the people (v3) reveal the shallowness of their professed knowledge of God.

The prophet Hosea next points out four areas of Israel's life in which Israel has proven false to God, thereby making his judgment certain. They are: false governments, gods, allies and altars.

1. False Governments (Hosea 8:4)

The setting up of kings as a substitute for God's rule goes back to the establishment of the monarchy (1 Sam 8:4-7).

Verse 4 refers to the rapid changes in Israel's ruling houses. In 200 years nineteen kings, representing nine separate dynasties, ruled. In the final 25 years (when Hosea was preaching) six kings from five separate dynasties ruled and four of the six were murdered by their successors.

2. False gods (Hosea 8:5-7)

Jeroboam Sacrificing to Idols, 1752, Jean Honoré Fragonard.

The references to the calf of Samaria in verses 5 and 6 are a reference to the bull pedestals erected by Jeroboam I about 920 BC at Bethel and Dan (1 Kings 12:25-33). Though originally these might not have been intended as objects of worship they became so in later Israelite practice and are continually condemned throughout the book of Kings. No doubt there were other idols used in Canaanite worship in Samaria also. For Old Testament thinking about idols read Isa 40:18-20; 41; 47:1-2, 5-7. Paul views idolatry as the basic sin of the pagan world which led to every other form of sin (Rom 1:20-32).

This proverbial saying, "Sowing the wind and reaping the whirlwind" is quoted to remind the Israelites that the judgment on them is the result of their own actions. The saying has a similar meaning to 'what you sow you will reap'.[1] In worshipping the calf and courting other nations, Israel has sown evil and so shall reap a harvest of destruction.

The second part of verse 7 is difficult. It seems to suggest that the grain standing in Israel's fields at the moment will not reach maturity but even if it did Israel would not enjoy it, for foreigners would devour it. In fact, already other nations have gobbled up Israel.

---
1   Dearman, *The Book of Hosea*, 227.

3. False Allies (Hosea 8:8-10)

Israel's appeal to the nations will prove futile. Already Israel is being swallowed up among the nations. Everything distinctive in Israel's way of life is gone. Israel's standing among them is no better than cheap useless pottery (v8). Israel's foreign alliances have robbed them of independence (v9-10) and soon Israel will lose all independence through being taken into exile (v10).

4. False Altars (Hosea 8:11-14)

Even those things designed originally to bring Israel nearer to God have the opposite effect. Altars, the symbol of devotion to God, have become the cause of sin either because they have been devoted to pagan sacrifice or to insincere worship (v11).

The true meaning of God's laws has been completely lost (v12). The people had shared their sacrificial meals and other forms of worship, and had thoroughly enjoyed themselves but the enjoyment had stopped there. Thus Hosea condemns priest and people for forgetting God and his moral requirements while they were zealously attending to every detail of their sacrificial worship. God does not accept this empty worship (v13). Instead, he will send them back to Egypt (v13) in the sense of a return to slavery as they were slaves in Egypt. All the effort they have put into the erection of elaborate buildings and fortifications will be wasted for these will be destroyed (v16); they ought to have remembered their Maker and trusted in him.

Hosea 9:1-6

This is apparently part of a sermon preached at some great harvest festival occasion. The prophet's message is a warning that people ought to refrain from the usual expressions of joy at such a festival because their pagan worship and immorality have brought God's judgment, and their rejoicing will be turned to mourning. Verses 1 & 2 may refer to immorality and drunkenness at the festivals or may be metaphorical descriptions of the unfaithfulness of the people. Verses 3-6 are developments of the thought of 8:13 where Egypt represents slavery, the actual exile being in Assyria.

Verses 4 and 5 emphasise the idea first expressed in 3:4 that in exile there will be no opportunity for festivals or sacrifice. Instead they will eat mourners' bread, that is food that is unclean and has not been blessed by involvement in sacrifice.

Hosea 9:7-9

The reaction of the people to Hosea's warning of judgment is to declare him to be a fool and a maniac but despite the opposition he encounters, even in the temple (v8), he reiterates his warning of coming judgment. The reference to Gibeah in verse 9 is an accusation that the disgraceful conduct of the Benjaminites in the story of Judg 19 is typical of the standards existing in Israel in the days in which he was preaching.

Hosea 9:10-17

When God chose Israel he is described as delighted as someone who finds grapes in the desert, or the first fruit on the tree. But even in the wilderness Israel had started to worship a Moabite version of the Baal cult (the story is told in Num 25:1-5). They have since continued in the worship of Baal until they have become as shameful as the thing they worship. (The text uses the word boset, shame, instead of the hated name of Baal, thereby showing how bad the people's apostasy from God was). The worst punishment God can bring on them is the loss of country, home and family (vv11-14).

Gilgal, condemned elsewhere (Amos 4:4; 5:5; Hos 4:15; 12:11), is chosen as a shrine which is representative of all forms of evil. This whole passage repeatedly plays on the meaning of Ephraim as 'fruitful' and this is strongly brought out in verse 16. Israel is condemned again to a life of exile (vv15,17).

Israel trusted in their favoured position as God's people to protect them while simultaneously trying to hedge their bets and obtain security from worldly powers and foreign gods. In their search for greater security they hastened their own destruction; a destruction that cost them their land, their autonomy, their connection to God, and was wrought by God using the very powers they looked to for protection.

Prayer

Dear Lord,

We bring before you those areas in our lives where we sin and sin again. We also ask you to examine us, to show us those areas where we haven't even realised our sin. Give us true repentance.

Amen

Topic 7 — Hosea 8—9

 Discussion Questions

1. The Israelites thought that they had turned to the Lord (8:2). How do we know this wasn't the case (8:3-6)?
2. Over the years, sin has been classified in a variety of ways (for example sins of omission versus sins of commission; knowing sin versus sin committed in ignorance; individual versus collective sin). List some of these categories and examples of the kinds of sin that they encompass.
3. List the various forms in which Israel's covenant breaking was expressed.
4. Festival days were to celebrate the Lord's goodness to Israel. Why then would God take away the joy of these celebrations in ch 9?
5. When do you find yourself focused more on God's blessings than on the God who blesses?
6. The prophets of God are rejected in chapter 9. How can we be receptive to God's messengers today?

 Demonstrate

What are the different false substitutes for God chosen by Israel, and why did they choose to trust in these rather than God?

 Notes: Topic 7

Hosea 8—9

Topic 8

Hosea 10

 ## Before we start

Hosea 10 is like a terribly beautiful poem of judgment, detailing the consequences of the people's idolatry. The dominating thought of this section is the consequences of putting your trust in anything or anyone else over God are disastrous.

 ## Study

Hosea 10:1-8

Verses 1 and 2 refer to this giving of credit to the Baals for the prosperity of the country. However, the emptiness of this worship will be shown when the symbols of it, the altars and the pillars, are broken down.

Israel's sin is centred in the charge, "Their heart is false" (NRSV v2). For the Hebrews, the heart was not the centre of not only emotion but also of will and intellect. Israel's problem then was one of commitment. Who has Israel's devotion, God or Baal? As a consequence of their divided or false hearts "they must suffer their sins", part of which punishment will be the destruction of altars and pillars so dear to them.

Verses 3 and 4 are concerned with the failure of the self-appointed monarchs to justify the people's trust. They are characterised by 'mere words' and 'empty oaths'. Jeroboam's calf at Bethel is equally a failure (vv5-6) and will bring tragedy, shame and finally exile to its people and priests alike.

The inhabitants of Samaria tremble for their golden calf. Instead of saving them, the calf becomes a source of anxiety to them; how can they save it? In the face of impending judgment people and priests mourn for its safety (and theirs). What can be so humiliating to a people as to have the god in whom they trust and whom they worship carried away captive? This will now happen to Israel. The false god to whom Israel brought offerings and rich gifts as tribute will in turn be offered as tribute to the king of Assyria (v6). The calf at Beth-aven (Bethel) is unable to save itself, how then can it save its worshippers? Israel will learn at last the futility and shame of setting up an idol as protector of the nation.

The false kings (v7) and the false worship (v8) face destruction and those who trust in them will be forced to such a point of desperation that in the end they will seek escape through their own destruction.

Hosea 10:9-15

Israel has never outgrown the kind of sin perpetrated at Gibeah (Judg 19, referred to in the last lesson). However, some scholars find in this reference to Gibeah the suggestion that Israel's present predicament actually originated with the initiation of kingship under Saul. Gibeah was Saul's place of residence during his kingship (see 1 Sam 10:26; 11:14). In this view, kingship on Israel's part was an effort to guarantee their future apart from God. As such, its establishment was evidence of a lack of faith in the sole leadership of God. Sin like this cannot go unpunished and the punishment will come as God gathers the nations to fight against Israel (vv9-10).

Shalmaneser V from Promptuarii Iconum Insigniorum (Guillaume Rouillé, 1553)

In verse 11 the picture changes. God's love for Israel has been expressed in the past in giving them an easy task in life, being like a heifer required only to walk round and round the threshing floor and able to eat as much as she liked. Now Israel must learn the more demanding tasks of ploughing and harrowing and must feel the harshness of the yoke; that is, Israel must be under someone's domination and direction. Compare this with the picture in the Garden of Eden, where the ease, good fellowship and freedom from harsh commands are followed by the unremitting toil outside the garden, the struggle of birth and life, and the estrangement between God and humanity.

Verse 12, speaking of God showering his righteousness, and coming as it does between verses 11 and 13 is like a welcome break in the clouds of the other verses.

Verse 11 describes the heavy yoke that Israel's sin has brought upon them, while verse 13 amplifies and elaborates the tragic results of the nations continued disobedience. In between there is found a word of hope and comfort, a warm appeal to return to God before it is too late.

Verse 12 is a call to repentance but it is repentance at the cost of effort. It requires breaking up ground long left fallow and the sowing of new qualities of righteousness and covenant loyalty. Previous expressions of repentance (6:1-3) have been too shallow, and only a costly change of character can result in God's blessing. By contrast with the righteousness Israel should be sowing, instead Israel has sown iniquity and must therefore reap the fruits of this seed (v13). Israel has chosen to put their trust in the weapons of war and will reap warfare and destruction (vv13-14).

The reference to Shalman in verse 14 is most probably Shalmaneser V who besieged Samaria in 722 BC, though the exact incident referred to here is difficult to identify. The Assyrians had a reputation for cruelty of which they boasted in their own inscriptions and no doubt the incident was well known to Hosea's hearers. The warning is clear enough. The Assyrians will destroy Israel and kill the king.

These chapters have included a series of short sermons with the recurring theme of the inevitability of divine judgment as their unifying bond. Perhaps the highlight of what is necessarily grim reading would be found in 10:11-12 with its promise that God will "train righteousness on the truly penitent." (NRSV)

Here we have seen the failure of those things we substitute for God to provide security and safety. We come to fear for the safety of our idols (particularly idols in the form of possessions) that we thought would make us feel secure and happy. The institutions we trust to protect us fail and break down. In the language of the playground - no matter how big our friends are, there is always someone bigger who can bully us and steal our lunch money.

The answer is to follow Jesus' advice:

Do not store up for yourselves treasures on earth, where moths and vermin destroy, and where thieves break in and steal. 20 But store up for yourselves treasures in heaven, where moths and vermin do not destroy, and where thieves do not break in and steal. 21 For where your treasure is, there your heart will be also.

Matt 6:19-21

We must put our trust in the one who is greater than all earthly powers, the one who no earthly powers are able to overcome.

Dear Lord,

Show us how we are operating out of fear, and instead let us to turn your perfect love, which casts out fear.

Amen

Hosea

 Discussion Questions

1. Who is shown to be in control in this chapter, and what does this mean for human power?

2. How is the plant metaphor used in this chapter to underscore how God overturns Israel's plans?

3. Read 1 Sam 8:1-9. Why did Israel want a king, and what was the warning? What has been the outcome in this chapter?

4. Israel is called to repentance. What will it cost them?

5. On the other hand, what will Israel gain from repentance (see vv11-12)?

6. How do we today find our security and hope in human power instead of in God?

 Demonstrate

What answer does chapter 10 give to those who suggest God is not sovereign? How do you understand sovereignty in a world where evil occurs?

 Notes: Topic 8

Hosea 10

Topic 9

Hosea 11–12

 ## Before we start

There is an ongoing debate regarding the role of jails and the extent to which they should be institutions of rehabilitation vs institutions of punishment. Some believe very strongly that jail should act as a deterrent to crime and should be as unpleasant and punitive as possible. Others, equally strongly, believe that people who are jailed should be given the opportunity to return to society better able to contribute than when they were removed from it. This basic conflict between the requirements of justice and mercy is apparent even in the heart of God, as God responds in love and holiness to our sin.

While there are still echoes of the coming judgment in these chapters there is now, clearly heard, the strong note of God's love for his people and the hope of ultimate salvation and restoration. Hosea's own experience of frustrated love gives him insight into the heart of God as the divine love for Israel is rebuffed and disregarded. The passages in these concluding chapters throb with the passion of divine love.

 Study

Hosea 11:1-4

Chapter 11 contains some of the most compassionate and tender verses in the entire book, and indeed the Old Testament. The picture is of God as parent. While this has often been assumed to be a Father, as Davies notes, these actions are more likely to be those of a mother.[1] The lovely picture of God caring for Israel is depicted delightfully in verse 3 where Israel as toddlers are taught to walk, picked up in their parent's arms and their bruises and sores tended. But the tragedy of such love is brought out in verse 2 where the entreaties of God's love are spurned and Israel's love is poured out on the Baalim. How much like that is Hosea's own experience with Gomer. In some translations of the Bible (NASB, ESV) verse 4 presents a different picture. Here God is a farmer who lovingly cares for animals, removing the bit from their mouths and easing the yoke from their shoulders after a day's work, personally feeding them, not driving them but lovingly leading them in their work. The verses are a tender picture of the solicitous love and consideration of God for beloved Israel.[2] Other translations (NRSV, NIV) have verse 4 continuing the loving parent theme. The original Hebrew is not clear. Either way, the loving care of God is unmistakable.

Hosea 11:5-7

With verse 5 there is a sudden change in tone in Hosea's message. Tender words of loving care are terminated and punishment is threatened. Despite God's love, Israel's sin cannot be passed over.

---

1   Graham I. Davies, *Hosea* (Sheffield: JSOT, 1993), 254.
2   See the discussion in Dearman, *The Book of Hosea*, 282-85.

Judgment will fall by way of exile (v5), warfare and invasion (v6). Although God wants to ease the yoke from them (v4) Israel's behaviour means he cannot do this and nor can anyone else (v7). Their yoke is, of course, service to another power in exile. Note the reiteration of the cause of judgment in verses 2, 5 and 7. "The more I called them, the more they went from me." (NRSV, v2).

Hosea 11:8-9

All this leads to God's frustrated cry of these verses. God cries "How can I give you up, Ephraim? How can I hand you over, Israel?" This heartrending cry expresses the undying love of a parent for a child. However, unworthy the child, the parent will never cease loving that child. The struggle within the very heart of God is intense; justice demands one thing, but mercy and love temper its demands. Smith comments on these verses that "they simply express the emotional intensity of God's love and anxiety in human terms that the audience can appreciate."[3] Admah and Zeboiim are either other names for Sodom and Gomorrah or else cities which suffered the same fate (Deut 29:23).

Because of his love, God exceeds the limits of covenant obligation and acts towards Israel in the realm of pure grace. How does God do this? The answer is found in God's own words, "for I am God and no mortal" (NRSV, v9). Contrary to humans, there is found with God that perfect union of love and grace which makes it possible for him not only to forgive but to discipline and recreate. This is what he did with Israel and continues to do with his people in every age, individually and collectively.

This deep and forgiving love of God does not remove the penalties of his judgment upon humanity; these are inescapable. However,

---

[3] Smith, *Hosea, Amos, Micah: The Niv Application Commentary from Biblical Text to Contemporary Life*, 163.

it does say to humanity that God's judgments, since they are controlled by love, are redemptive and disciplinary rather than punitive and destructive.

Hosea 11:10-11

Here the prophet looks beyond the exile to the moment when God's love will finally be returned by Israel and they will return from their exile. The lion's roar may be used as a symbol to strike terror or in the sense of a call of the lion to his young. In the latter case they come trembling in the sense of eagerness, in the former, in fear. The general sense of the verses is clear. After a necessary period of punishment in exile Israel will be restored by God to their own land. Compare Hos 3:5 and 2:14-23.

Hosea 11:12-12:14

Gustave Doré, Jacob Wrestling with the Angel (1855)

A return is made in these verses to the sins of Israel and Judah and a brief review is made of some historical incidents to show that deceit and sin were always evident in the nation's history. Instead of looking to ancient events for the sole purpose of showing the early and continuing character of Israel's sin (compare with 9:10, 15; 10:9), Hosea presents episodes in the life of a patriarchal ancestor Jacob for the purpose of exhorting Israel to act in the same way.

Israel has surrounded God with deceit (v12). Israel (Ephraim) "feeds on the wind; he pursues the east wind all day" (12:1), that is, engages in useless tasks. The east wind may be a reference to the hot wind off the desert which is unpleasant and to be avoided.[4]

Verses 2 to 4 contain a reference to Jacob, whose name is a play on the words for grasping (the heel) and deceiving, both of which are seen in his story (see Gen 25:19-34, 27:35-36).[5] Verses 3b and 4 suggest the other side to Jacob's nature; the struggle with God at Peniel (Gen 32:24-32) and the revelation at Bethel (Gen 28:10-22) are evidence of Jacob's personal encounters with God. So Israel is called on, like Jacob, to renew personal contact with God, but unlike him, to observe fair dealings with others (v6).

This reference to the history of the patriarch Jacob, serves as a warning and an exhortation to Israel. The nation is warned of the deep-rooted nature of its love for lies and its dealings in deceit, and of the necessity to cease from such betrayal of their covenant relationship with God. At the same time, this reference is an exhortation to the nation as Hosea pointed to Jacob as the one who through weeping and supplication found strength and favour with God. This could be theirs if they would return to God, demonstrate love and justice to others "and wait patiently for your God to act" (v6).

Ethical conduct is lacking in Israel where dishonest practices have resulted in great wealth, but this wealth is unable to cover their sins (vv7-8). God will discipline Israel by a return to the restrictions and privations of the wilderness life, away from the luxuries of their wealth and its attendant evils (v9). The wilderness is often thought of as the ideal period (compare with Hos 2:14) when God and Israel were in genuine union. In Israel's past it had been through the prophets that God has revealed his will and led his people (vv10, 13 – the reference is to Moses). Now the prophetic

---

[4] Dearman, *The Book of Hosea*, 298.
[5] Smith, *Hosea, Amos, Micah: The Niv Application Commentary from Biblical Text to Contemporary Life*, 172-73.

Hosea

ministry has been rejected and in its place is the worship of Gilead and Gilgal with its pagan and polluted sacrifice. But this will prove to be completely ineffective when trouble comes and the symbols of such worship will be destroyed (v11).

In verse 12 Hosea again refers to the example of Jacob. The historical threat broken off at verse 6 is resumed. Verses 12 and 13 contrast the hard lot of Jacob in one of his experiences, namely looking for a wife, and that of Israel in their deliverance from Egypt and entrance into the land of promise. Jacob served almost as a slave for wife (or both wives, see Gen 27-29). In contrast God delivered Israel from Egypt by a prophet and gave the nation its rich heritage as a gift. After they were in the land God continued to provide and care for them, but what was Israel's attitude and response? Instead of gratitude to God for his blessings, Israel provoked God to anger with disobedience and idolatry. Therefore, Israel will bear the consequences of their own guilt (v14).

The sin of Israel creates a conflict in the heart of God between his love for Israel and the justice of his character. God feels intense pain over the discipline he must give, but his great love for Israel will temper his acts of judgment so that they become acts of discipline aimed at restoration. God wishes his people to be reconciled to him like Jacob, but also to be free from the idolatry and injustice caused by wealth.

Prayer

Dear Lord,

Help us to understand the parental nature of God's love for us, that he both disciplines us but also forgives us, and desperately desires us to be reconciled with him.

Amen

Topic 9 — Hosea 11—12

# Discussion Questions

1. What does the metaphor of God teaching Israel to walk reveal?
2. In what way is God not like a human (11:9), and how is this comforting and challenging?
3. In Chapter 12, what contrast is made between Israel and God?
4. In what does Israel find security in instead of God in chapter 12?
5. How do discipline and mercy work together to transform people?
6. How is Christ illustrated and foreshadowed in this section of Hosea's prophecy?

# Demonstrate

What do you learn about God and relationship with his people from the parent metaphor of chapter 11? (compare with 2 other references to God as parent in the Old Testament)

 Notes: Topic 9

Hosea 11—12

Topic 10

Hosea 13–14

Before we start

There is no doubt that the fullest expression of God's love is found in the person of Jesus Christ. In Christ we see the final reconciliation of God's justice and mercy. Jesus took upon himself the punishment we were due and as we examine these last two chapters of Hosea we will see God's great sacrifice on our behalf foreshadowed.

Study

Hosea 13—14

Chapter 13 serves well as a summary of much that has gone before. The early promise of Israel and God's tender care; Israel's forgetfulness and apostasy; the failure of kings and the stubborn sin of the people; and finally the inevitability of the coming judgment. This is indeed a dark chapter, for it contains the prospect of unmitigated doom and destruction, the death knell for the nation.[1]

---

1   See the discussion of this issue in Dearman, *The Book of Hosea,* 318-19.

Hosea 13:1-3

Again judgment is the theme, the specific cause being Israel's idolatry both with the Baals and Jeroboam's calves. God will sweep them away as something of no substance (v3).

Hosea describes the circumstances by which Ephraim fell from favour and died. It isn't clear here whether Ephraim is the man, the tribe or is operating as a synonym for the nation. It seems to best fit the context that this is the tribe, whose fate gives a warning to the nation. Ephraim's death warrant was due to idolatry. The Israel of Hosea's day is no better than the Ephraim of old. The nation had accelerated its pace of sinning against God: from a perverted worship of God through the figure of the calf, they had moved to worship the idol itself. Then they increased their sin by making metal images and by expressing their devotion by kissing the calves.

Hosea 13:4-11

Illustration of Jeroboam setting up two golden calves, Bible Historiale, 1372.

Israel is reminded of God's love and provision in the past, especially in the wilderness period, but Israel's response is heartbreakingly the same. Having obtained what they wanted from him they forgot God (vv4-6). God's reaction is described in the graphic picture of the wild beast who tears its prey to pieces (vv7-8). Nothing can save Israel (v9) not even their kings, whom Israel had asked for (1 Sam 8) and to whom they looked for so much are powerless. The frequent turnover of monarch had not just been due to human machinations but was also evidence of God's anger (vv9-11).

Hosea 13:12-16

In verse 12 Hosea assures Israel that none of their sin will be forgotten. The picture is that of a book which is bound up for further reference. In quite a different image in verse 13 Israel is described as an unborn child who is powerless to be born at the very moment when birth is in process. Any such foetus which doesn't come forth from the womb, whatever the cause, faces certain death. God's prophets on numerous occasions had proclaimed to Israel the possibilities of a new life and had set forth the manner of entering into it, but the nation had stubbornly refused to enter. When an individual or a nation refuses life, the only alternative is death.

So Israel has failed to repent when the opportunity presented itself. Now only destruction awaits them. In verse 14 the prophet's point is clear. There is a limit to the patience of God, he will no longer show compassion to Israel. So the Lord will not ransom them from the power of Sheol, or redeem them from death. Instead he calls upon both Sheol (world of the dead) and death to do their worst against Israel.

The threat of destruction is carried further in verses 15 and 16 where the invading Assyrians are described as a blasting east wind which dries up all in its path, and the gruesome barbarities of the invasion are depicted.

Hosea 14:1-9

The whole tone of the prophecy alters in this final chapter and hope of repentance and restoration burns bright. The chapter is so different from what precedes it that many critics want to credit it to some other author but this is to deny the persistently recurring suggestions of hope that are present throughout the prophecy and the underlying story of Gomer's restitution to Hosea. Surely Hosea who saw so clearly the nature of God's persistent redeeming love must also see the hope of such love triumphing even through pain and necessary judgment.

Hosea has used numerous genres in his prophecies. As Stuart suggests this last chapter "recalls the penitential psalms".[2] The whole passage and verse 9 provides an excellent conclusion and an appropriate summary of the prophet's message to Israel.

Israel needs to return to God with an honest confession of sin and a willingness to change their attitude to idols and foreign alliances (vv1-3). Therefore, when Israel repents and comes before God, instead of Canaanite sacrifices and idol worship Israel will offer sincere words of confession and supplication - words indicative of heartfelt repentance (v20). Such an attitude is assured of the forgiveness of God and his blessing on their land (vv4-6).

Hosea makes use of metaphors drawn from nature in verses 5-8. God will be "as rain in a dry land", which represents that which refreshes and renews life. God will be to his repentant people as the refreshing dew or rain, reviving them as the abundant dew of Palestine revives vegetation withered by a burning sun. Then Israel, in the right relationship with God, will grow luxuriantly. The entire picture is one of renewal, life, growth, beauty and productivity - all of which are the results of repentance.

As the NRSV translates verse 8, it becomes a final cry from God to Israel to understand his nature and realise it was he who cared and provided for them. In the divine response to Israel's repentance, God has said, "I am like an evergreen cypress" (v8). The simile's main emphasis is on the tree's continuing greenness,

---

[2] Douglas K. Stuart, *Hosea-Jonah*, Word Biblical Themes (Dallas: Word Pub., 1989), 212.

undiminished by changing seasons. The evergreen is referred to not so much as a particular species or type, but as indicative of that which is constantly alive. In God alone then will Israel find true life.

The final verse of the prophecy may have been added later by an editor. Whatever the case, it is a fitting conclusion to the book, calling for reflection on the teaching of the book and asserting faith in the ultimate justice and righteousness of God. Human hope and help reside in the God who, in spite of humanity's stubborn refusal to be upright and walk in his ways, still loves and forgives.

These last two chapters present both a stark warning and a great hope. God will judge, both the world and also his chosen people. But when human beings truly repent they will find blessing. The faithful, unconditional love of God for sinful human beings knows no greater expression than in God's willingness to send his own Son, Jesus, to suffer and die in our place, so that we are able to enjoy the love of God forever.

Prayer

Dear Lord,

It is our prayer that you will motivate us and enable us to go to the world with your message of reconciliation.

Amen

 ## Discussion Questions

1. Why does God react like a wild beast? What did the nation do to provoke this?
2. Why does Hosea remind Israel of God's provision for them in the past?
3. What metaphors of renewal does Hosea draw from nature?
4. What is the result of Israel's sin (13:15-16)? What is the ultimate aim this do you think?
5. Israel turned to other places of security instead of the one true God. What do we learn about God from chapter 14 that reiterates why trust should be put in God instead?
6. The end of Hosea reminds us that the wise both understand and walk in the ways of the Lord – how do you get this balance right?

 ## Demonstrate

What is the central message of Hosea? How would you relate this to the church today?

 Notes: Topic 10

Hosea 13—14

List of References

Davies, Graham I. *Hosea.* Sheffield: JSOT, 1993.

Dearman, J. Andrew. *The Book of Hosea*. The New International Commentary on the Old Testament. Grand Rapids, Michigan: Eerdmans, 2010.

Garrett, Duane A. *Hosea, Joel.* The New American Commentary. Nashville, Tennessee: Broadman & Holman, 1997.

Smith, Gary V. *Hosea, Amos, Micah: The Niv Application Commentary from Biblical Text to Contemporary Life.* The Niv Application Commentary Series. Grand Rapids, Mich.: Zondervan Pub. House, 2001.

Stuart, Douglas K. *Hosea-Jonah*. Word Biblical Themes. Dallas: Word Pub., 1989.

Strongs Exhaustive Concordance. http://www.biblestudytools.com/concordances/strongs-exhaustive-concordance/

www.ingramcontent.com/pod-product-compliance
Lightning Source LLC
Chambersburg PA
CBHW050543300426
44113CB00012B/2244